Fact Finders®

PEOPLE YOU
SHOULD KNOW

JOHN LEWIS

Get to Know the Statesman Who Marched for Civil Rights

by Jehan Jones-Radgowski

CAPSTONE PRESS
a capstone imprint

Fact Finders Books are published by Capstone Press,
1710 Roe Crest Drive, North Mankato, Minnesota 56003
www.mycapstone.com

Library of Congress Cataloging-in-Publication Data
Library of Congress Cataloging-in-Publication data is available on
the Library of Congress website.

ISBN 978-1-5435-5525-7 (library binding)
ISBN 978-1-5435-5924-8 (paperback)
ISBN 978-1-5435-5536-3 (eBook PDF)

Editorial Credits
Mari Bolte, editor; Kayla Rossow, designer; Svetlana Zhurkin, media researcher;
Tori Abraham, production specialist

Photo Credits
Alabama Department of Archives and History: Donated by Alabama Media Group/Photo by Robert Adams or Norman Dean, Birmingham News, 8; AP Photo: 27, BHR, 4, Matt Slocum, cover; Getty Images: Hulton Archive/Express/William Lovelace, 5, Keystone-France/Gamma-Keystone, 12, New York Times Co., 22, The LIFE Picture Collection/Don Cravens, 18, The LIFE Picture Collection/Francis Miller, 25, The LIFE Picture Collection/Grey Villet, 19, The LIFE Picture Collection/Paul Schutzer, 7, The LIFE Picture Collection/Robert W. Kelley, 11, The Washington Post/Gerald Martineau, 21, Villon Films/Robert Elfstrom, 26; Library of Congress, 6, 14, 17, 24; Newscom: CNP/Ron Sachs, 28; Shutterstock: KennStilger47, 23
Design Elements by Shutterstock

Source Notes
p. 11, line 6: John Lewis and Andrew Aydin. *March: Book One*. Marietta, Georgia: Top Shelf Productions, 2013, p. 49.
p. 12, line 4: John Lewis. *Walking With the Wind: A Memoir of the Movement*. New York: Simon & Schuster, 1998, p. 39.
p. 13, line 7: *March: Book One*, p. 54.
p. 14, line 4: Andrew Albanese. "ALA 2013: The Day Congressman John Lewis Got His Library Card." https://www.publishersweekly.com/pw/by-topic/digital/conferences/article/58040-ala-2013-the-day-congressman-john-lewis-got-his-library-card.html. Accessed 15 August 2018.
p. 15, line 7: Joshua Berlinger. "Rep. John Lewis Goes Bac to His Roots." https://www.cnn.com/2016/06/23/politics/john-lewis-sit-ins/index.html. Accessed 12 August 2018.
p. 15, sidebar, line 6: Amnesty International. "15 Powerful Martin Luther King, Jr. Quotes."https://www.amnestyusa.org/15-powerful-martin-luther-king-jr-quotes/. Accessed 12 August 2018.
p. 19, line 1: U.S. History. "Rosa Parks and the Montgomery Bus Boycott."http://www.ushistory.org/us/54b.asp. Accessed 14 September 2018.
p. 20, line 15: CBS News. "Note to Self: Congressman John Lewis on the 'moral obligation' to 'speak up'." https://www.cbsnews.com/news/note-to-self-congressman-john-lewis-civil-rights-leader/. Accessed 14 September 2018.
p. 22, line 11: Wesley Lowery. "John Lewis Recalls First Meeting with MLK and an Apology from a Klansman." https://www.washingtonpost.com/news/post-nation/wp/2015/02/27/john-lewis-recalls-first-meeting-mlk-and-an-apology-from-a-klansman/?utm_term=.aeac4d488779. Accessed 19 September 2018.
p. 29, line 10: Sophia Nguyen. "Lewis on Leadership: Faust's Farewell." https://www.harvardmagazine.com/2018/05/commencement-john-lewis. Accessed 10 August 2018.

Printed in the United States of America.
PA48

TABLE OF CONTENTS

1 ▷ FREEDOM RIDER

On May 4, 1961, 22-year-old John Lewis waited for a bus in Washington, D.C. He and 12 men and women, both black and white, would ride two buses to New Orleans, Louisiana. The riders would later be known as the Freedom Riders. Their goal was to break long-held practices of **discrimination**.

At bus stations, they would ignore "Whites Only" signs. They would sit together where they could. Doing this meant they risked being stopped, arrested, or attacked by angry mobs. But they vowed to resist peacefully. If they were arrested, they would not pay fines or post **bail**. If they faced violence, they would not return it.

the Freedom Riders review a map of a bus route

Two Lanes

For nearly 100 years, African Americans had experienced **segregation** while traveling. They could not sit in the front of buses. Black and white people had separate places to wait at bus or train stations. But on June 3, 1946, the United States Supreme Court ruled against segregated seating on buses that traveled interstate. And in December 1960, they added bathrooms, waiting rooms, lunch counters, and any other facility associated with interstate travel to that ruling.

However, rulings were often ignored, especially in the southern United States. Many white Southerners refused to integrate, believing that people should be separated based on their skin color.

discrimination—treating people unfairly because of their race, country of birth, gender, or religion

bail—a sum of money paid to a court to allow someone accused of a crime to be set free until his or her trial

segregation—the practice of keeping groups of people apart, especially based on race

The riders passed quietly through Virginia. But in Charlotte, North Carolina, Joe Perkins asked for a shoeshine at a whites-only shoeshine chair. He was arrested, and the other riders had to continue on without him.

Six days into the trip, the bus stopped in Rock Hill, South Carolina. John was attacked as he tried to enter a whites-only waiting room. In Winnsboro, black Riders were arrested at a whites-only lunch counter.

The Freedom Riders escaped the bus, but many suffered from smoke inhalation.

On May 14, the buses passed through Anniston, Alabama. One was attacked on the road. Windows were smashed and tires were slashed. A firebomb was thrown on board. The bus caught fire. The Riders tried to escape, but the doors were blocked. Someone yelled, "Burn them alive!" When they ran off the bus, the attackers waited outside.

The second bus made it to the station. An angry mob boarded the bus and beat the passengers. The driver made it to Birmingham, Alabama, but the Riders were attacked there too. Jim Peck needed 53 stitches. Walter Bergman suffered permanent brain damage after being beaten.

Ticket to Ride

The 13 Freedom Riders were John Lewis, Joe Perkins, Jim Peck, Elton Cox, Walter Bergman, Frances Bergman, Jimmy McDonald, Charles Person, Ed Blankenheim, Genevieve Hughes, Albert Bigelow, Hank Thomas, and James Farmer. Farmer was the group's leader.

The Freedom Riders gathered in a church in Montgomery, Alabama, in 1961. John Lewis is in the front row, second from the right.

Even after everything that had happened, the Riders wanted to go on. Unfortunately, there was not a bus driver willing to take them. The Freedom Ride was delayed until May 17. John and Hank Thomas organized another group to travel from Nashville, Tennessee, to Birmingham.

When they reached Birmingham, police arrested them. That night, they were driven to the Tennessee border and left in the middle of nowhere. On foot and afraid, they got back to Birmingham and boarded a bus to Montgomery, Alabama. They were met by more violence there. John was hit over the head with a wooden crate.

Police arrested Charles Butler (left) and John (right) at the station in Birmingham.

On May 24 the Riders rode to Jackson, Mississippi, with an escort of National Guardsmen. Even so, they were arrested again. They were sent to a maximum security facility and spent 39 days in prison.

By this time, people all over the world had heard about the Freedom Riders and what they went through. In the fall of 1961 separate facilities based on race in bus and train terminals finally ended.

John had proven he was willing to risk everything for equality. But it was only the beginning of his battle.

DID YOU KNOW?

After John's famous ride, more than 400 other volunteers from across 40 states joined the Freedom Riders. They trained for several days. They learned local and state laws regarding segregation and their rights as citizens. They also learned what they could legally do if their rights were denied.

2 > EARLY YEARS

John Lewis was born in Troy, Alabama, on February 21, 1940. His parents, Eddie and Willie Mae, were poor farmers. They grew corn, peanuts, and cotton. John had nine brothers and sisters. Everyone had to help on the farm. When John was young, his main job was to take care of the chickens. He treated them like special pets. He would read the Bible, the family's only book, to them.

There was only one school for black children in John's town. There were two rooms for all the students. There was no running water or indoor plumbing. In the winter John and his friends searched for sticks and branches to burn in the tiny stove. Everything in the school was homemade or bought by the community. On rainy days, the old bus they rode would get stuck in the mud. The students would have to get off and push it to school.

On the way to his school, John's bus passed buses and schools for white children. The buses were shiny and traveled on paved roads. The whites-only schools were new and had playgrounds. John also noticed something else. "We drove past prison work gangs almost every day," he said. "The prisoners were always black. As were the folks working in the fields beyond them. You couldn't help but notice."

John could only go to school when there was no work to do. But he wanted to learn. Sometimes he would jump on the bus even though he knew he was needed at home.

When John was 11, he took a trip with his uncle to New York. Going from the segregated South to the **integrated** North was shocking. John said arriving in New York "was like stepping into a movie, into a strange, otherworldly place." He was shocked to see white and black people living in the same neighborhoods. This visit convinced John that people of different races could—and should—live, play, and study together.

children playing in Harlem, a neighborhood in New York City, in 1950

John wasn't the only one who thought this way. In the summer of 1954 the Supreme Court ruled on *Brown v. Board of Education*. They said that separating schools by race was **unconstitutional**. Schools were to integrate as soon as possible. John was excited for the change. "I thought that, come fall, I'd be riding a state-of-the-art bus to a state-of-the-art school," he said. "An integrated school."

But things did not change in Alabama and in other southern states. The leaders of John's state did not obey the Supreme Court's ruling. Life continued as it had before—segregated.

Not Equal

"Separate but equal" was a phrase used to describe the segregation system in most southern states. The idea was that separating groups by race was good for the community. As long as all children received the same education, it shouldn't matter. But the education white children received was often much better. Their schools were better funded, better constructed, and better supplied. There was very little that was truly equal.

integrate—to bring people of different races together in schools and other public places

unconstitutional—a law that goes against something set forth in the Constitution

13

3 ▶ RESISTANCE

John knew that segregation was wrong. He also knew that the idea that some people were better than others because of the color of their skin is wrong. "I would come home and ask my mother, my father, my grandparents, my great grandparents, why? They'd say accept what is, don't get in the way, don't get in trouble." One day things would be better. But John didn't want to wait.

a black moviegoer entering the colored entrance of a segregated movie theater in Mississippi

The year 1955 was a landmark one for John. The voice of a powerful preacher from Atlanta, Georgia, rang out over the radio. This preacher's style of speaking and his commanding voice made John stop and listen. His sermon urged people to fight to make their lives better. "It seemed like Martin Luther King Jr. was speaking directly to me, saying John Lewis, you too can do something. You can make a contribution."

MLK

Martin Luther King Jr. (MLK) was an activist and a minister. He played a key role in the Civil Rights movement. He had a leading role in the nonviolent protest movement. He also spoke out against the Vietnam War (1955–1975), poverty, and inequality. He was **assassinated** in 1968.

"In the end, we will remember not the words of our enemies, but the silence of our friends."
–Martin Luther King Jr.

assassinate—to murder a person who is well-known or important

Other events moved John to speak up. That fall, 14-year-old Emmett Till was viciously murdered after a white woman said he flirted with her. Fifteen-year-old John realized that the same thing could happen to him or to any of his family or friends. He was angry at the system that allowed black men and boys to die. He was angry that he couldn't do anything to stop it.

On December 1 a woman named Rosa Parks was arrested while riding a public bus. The bus had a "white" section and a "colored" section. Rosa was sitting in the "colored" section, but rules stated that white riders had a right to a seat if the bus was full. A white man wanted her seat. Rosa was tired. She refused to move.

DID YOU KNOW?

Rosa Parks was not the first bus passenger to refuse to give up her seat. Residents of Montgomery had been fighting for bus equality since 1954. Claudette Colvin and Mary Louise Smith were also arrested for the same reason.

Rosa Parks was arrested and fined. She refused to pay. Later, both she and her husband lost their jobs.

Signed Into Law

In 2007 the Emmett Till Unsolved Civil Rights Crime Act was passed. The act gave the U.S. Department of Justice (DOJ) and the Federal Bureau of Investigation (FBI) the ability to explore murders involving unsolved civil rights violations that happened earlier than 1970. In 2016 it was expanded to include events before 1980. In 2017 Till's accuser, Carolyn Bryant, admitted that she had lied. In March 2018 the DOJ re-opened the case.

Rosa was the secretary of the local chapter of the National Association for the Advancement of Colored People (NAACP). She was tired of discriminatory rules. Local leaders called for a **boycott** of buses in Montgomery.

The boycott began on December 5. African Americans made up about 75 percent of all the bus riders in the city. More than 90 percent of them stayed off the buses that day. The boycott was such a success that the organizers decided to keep it going.

In total, about 40,000 African American passengers boycotted buses on December 5.

boycott—to refuse to take part in something as a way of making a protest

Some boycotters walked 3 to 5 miles (4.8 to 8 kilometers) rather than ride the bus.

"Don't ride the buses to work, to town, to school, or anywhere. . . . If you work, take a cab, or share a ride, or walk," a leaflet advised. Black taxi drivers lowered their fares to 10 cents, the same price as the bus. Other people worked out carpool schedules to get to and from work, walked, or rode a bike. The boycott lasted for 13 months and was the first large-scale demonstration in the United States against segregation.

On November 23, 1956, the Supreme Court ruled that bus segregation went against the U.S. Constitution. The boycott had worked.

19

The boycott was inspiring to 16-year-old John, who had followed its every move in the news. So when it was time to make his own protest, he was ready.

John had gone to the Pike County Public Library and tried to apply for a library card. The library was for white people only, and the librarian refused his application. John went home and wrote a **petition**. He argued that black people should be able to use the public library too. He asked all his schoolmates and friends to sign their names. Then he mailed the appeal to the library.

The librarian never responded, but John was proud of his first act of defiance. "When you see something that is not right, not fair, not just, you have a moral obligation to continue to speak up, to speak out," he said later.

petition—a letter signed by many people asking leaders for a change

The First Sit-In

In 1939 a man named Samuel Tucker staged the first sit-in in the United States. His local library in Alexandria, Virginia, had been built with taxpayer money—from both black and white taxpayers—but was open for whites only. Tucker recruited five other young black men for the sit-in. They were arrested and taken to court. The following January, a judge ruled that the city could not deny its black citizens the right to use a library. The city answered by building a library for black patrons down the street. This library was not as nice, but the city could argue that everyone now had library access. Tucker's library was not **desegregated** until 1960.

The five men who participated in Tucker's sit-in entered the library and quietly began to read. They were arrested for disorderly conduct.

DID YOU KNOW?

In 1998 John wrote a book called *Walking With the Wind*. That year he visited the Pike County Public Library for a book signing. Afterward, the library gave him the card he had been denied in 1956.

sit-in—form of protest in which demonstrators refuse to leave a place

desegregate—to get rid of any laws or practices that separate people of different races

In 1957 John graduated high school and wanted to go to college. He had applied to a school nearby—a whites-only school. He never heard back. So he wrote another letter—this time to Martin Luther King Jr. "I told him I needed his help," John said.

Martin Luther King Jr. rose in the activist community after being elected spokesman for the Montgomery bus boycott.

By the time MLK wrote back, John had been accepted at American Baptist College in Nashville, Tennessee. MLK still wanted to see him. He sent John a bus ticket and told him to join him in Montgomery. The meeting between MLK and the "Boy from Troy" was monumental.

John graduated from American Baptist College in 1961 and Fisk University (below) in 1967.

DID YOU KNOW?

MLK said he would help John sue the college that had rejected him. But he also told John that it would be dangerous. His parents could lose their land, or be threatened. After thinking it over, John decided not to sue.

While studying in Nashville, John got more involved in the civil rights movement. One of his first acts of large-scale resistance was the Nashville sit-in movement. Black and white students joined together to protest the fact that black people could not eat at lunch counters in the city. Each day, dressed in their best clothes, they visited the restaurants and stores in downtown Nashville. They sat at the lunch counters and waited.

Between February 1961 and the end of that school year, more than 1,500 black protesters had been arrested at sit-ins.

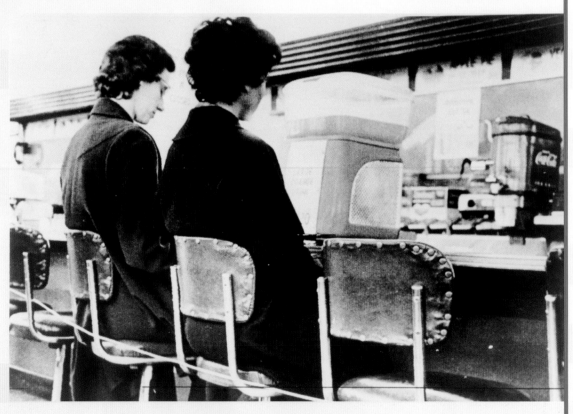

Each day, the waiters and managers refused to serve them. Sometimes the restaurants would close and turn off the lights, with the protesters still inside. Sometimes angry people yelled at them to leave the restaurant, poured ketchup on their hair and clothing, or hit them. But the protesters didn't budge.

After several months of sit-ins, the restaurants finally agreed to serve black people.

John (third from left) leading a protest march in 1967

Nonviolent Dreams

John Lewis continued his nonviolent protests with the Freedom Rides of 1960. In 1963 John became the chairman of the Student Nonviolent Coordinating Committee (SNCC). That same year, he helped plan the March on Washington. At 23 years old, he was the youngest of the organizers. On August 28, more than 250,000 people gathered in front of the Lincoln Memorial in Washington, D.C. John gave a speech that day, although MLK's "I Have a Dream" speech is the one that most people remember.

25

John in an office in
New York City, 1964

In 1965 John organized a peaceful protest in Selma, Alabama. The protesters wanted to improve voter rights in the state. While black people had the ability to vote, obstacles had been put in place by white lawmakers to make it difficult for them to do so.

The first protest took place on March 7, 1965. John planned to march from Selma to Montgomery. As they crossed the bridge just outside Selma, Alabama state troopers demanded they turn around. Those who did not do so were beaten by police officers. Tear gas was thrown at them. Many of the marchers were injured. John's skull was fractured.

Journalists were there to capture the event. They called it "Bloody Sunday." News stations broadcast the images around the world. People were horrified to see violence used against peaceful protesters.

Later there were two more marches. John, MLK, and hundreds of supporters finally made it across the bridge and into Montgomery on the third try.

DID YOU KNOW?

John was one of the "Big Six" leaders of the civil rights movement. The other five are MLK, James Farmer, A. Philip Randolph, Roy Wilkins, and Whitney Young. John is the only leader still alive today.

IT'S A MOVEMENT

Bloody Sunday was a turning point in the civil rights movement. President Lyndon B. Johnson signed the Voting Rights Act on August 6, 1965. It prohibited racial discrimination in voting.

In 1977 the congressman in Georgia's 5th congressional district was made an ambassador. This meant his spot in Congress was empty. John ran for the office. He lost, but continued his work in civil rights. In 1981 he served on the Atlanta City Council. He ran for Congress again in 1986 and won. He has been re-elected in every election since, winning by wide margins every time.

John's work paved the way for President Barack Obama to be elected in 2008 and again in 2012.

In 2011 President Barack Obama awarded John the Presidential Medal of Freedom, the highest award given to a civilian. In 2013 John wrote *March*, the first book in a three-book graphic novel series about his work in civil rights.

John continues his work fighting for the rights of others. He wants children today to fight too. "You must lead," he said. "You're never too young to lead, you're never too old to lead. We need your leadership now more than ever before."

DID YOU KNOW?

John was arrested in 2013 for the 45th time. He was at a rally to protest an immigrant reform bill. Seven other members of Congress were arrested too.

Remember the Past

In 1988 John introduced the idea of a museum dedicated to black history. In 2016 his dream became a reality. The National Museum of African American History and Culture opened its doors in Washington, D.C., on September 24.

GLOSSARY

assassinate (us-SASS-uh-nate)—to murder a person who is well-known or important

bail (BAYL)—a sum of money paid to a court to allow someone accused of a crime to be set free until his or her trial

boycott (BOY-kot)—to refuse to take part in something as a way of making a protest

desegregate (dee-seg-ruh-GAYT)—to get rid of any laws or practices that separate people of different races

discrimination (dis-kri-muh-NAY-shuhn)—treating people unfairly because of their race, country of birth, gender, or religion

integrate (IN-tuh-grate)—to bring people of different races together in schools and other public places

petition (puh-TISH-uhn)—a letter signed by many people asking leaders for a change

segregation (seg-ruh-GAY-shuhn)—the practice of keeping groups of people apart, especially based on race

sit-in (SIT-IN)—form of protest in which demonstrators refuse to leave a place, such as a place of business or government building

unconstitutional (un-kon-stuh-TOO-shuhn-uhl)—a law that goes against something set forth in the Constitution, the document that set up the government of the United States

READ MORE

Fishman, Jon M. *Martin Luther King Jr.: Walking In the Light*. Minneapolis: Lerner Publications, 2019.

Lewis, John, and Andrew Aydin. *March: Book One*. Marietta, Georgia: Top Shelf Productions, 2013.

Llanas, Sheiila. *Children in the Civil Rights Era*. Mendota Heights, Minn.: Focus Readers, 2018.

INTERNET SITES

Use FactHound to find Internet sites related to this book.

Visit *www.facthound.com*

Just type in 9781543555257 and go.

Check out projects, games and lots more at
www.capstonekids.com

CRITICAL THINKING QUESTIONS

1. Have you ever experienced something that you felt was unfair? What did you do about it? What do you wish you had done differently?

2. Name someone who has inspired you. What causes do they stand for? List the way or ways they have fought for change.

3. How was your childhood different than John's? Name a few differences. Then list some similarities. How have your experiences shaped your life?

INDEX